The Craft of Temari

The Craft of Temari

Mary Wood

SEARCH PRESS

First published in Great Britain 1991
Search Press Limited,
Wellwood, North Farm Road,
Tunbridge Wells, Kent TN2 3DR
Reprinted 1994

ISBN 0 85532 653 0 (Pb)

Acknowledgements
The author would like to thank Suzuko Anai for
introducing her to the craft of temari and providing her
with English notes on the history of the subject; Kiyoharu
Tanami of Macaw Publishing Company for supplying her
with books in Japanese; Jan Messent for her expert advice
and encouragement; her husband Jim, and daughters
Amanda and Philippa, for their support and patience; and
her many students and friends for allowing her to use
their temari, especially Dorothy Atkins, Ruth Baldwin,
Betty Garrard, Sylvia Hold, Janet Martin, Colleen Nichol,
Jeanette Peake and Joan Sterry.

Composition by Genesis Typesetting, Rochester, Kent
Colour Separation by P & W Graphics Pte Ltd
Printed and bound in Malaysia

Contents

Introduction
6

Equipment and materials
9

How to begin
12
Making the basic mari · Colour · Embroidery threads
Beads and sequins · Dividing the basic mari
Putting in the marker threads

Simple temari designs
20
Wrapping and stitching

SIMPLE DIVISION
Squares · Rose garden · Spindles · Crossed spindles
Interlocking spindles · Three wing and hexagon
Three wing · Pentagon · Interlocking diamonds
Chrysanthemum

WRAPPED DESIGNS
Design 1 · Design 2 · Design 3 · Design 4

Complex temari designs
52

EIGHT COMPLEX DIVISION
Dividing into eight sections · Rose garden
Chrysanthemum · Three wing and hexagon
Wrapped designs · Interlocking triangles
Woven squares

TEN COMPLEX DIVISION
Dividing into ten sections · Interlocking pentagons
Chrysanthemum · Rose garden

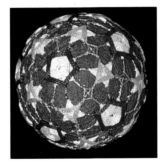

Introduction

The history of this fascinating craft goes back to the eighth century when a ball game called *kemari (ke* means kicking) was imported into Japan from China. The ball was made of deerskin and the game was played by noblemen of the Imperial Court. They kicked the ball high in the air and then caught it with their feet, but eventually the game developed and the ball was thrown and caught by hand. There is some uncertainty as to when the ball game became part of popular culture, but, in the fourteenth to sixteenth centuries, street performers were known to use balls for juggling.

It was around this time also that temari, as we know them today, came into being. The female servants of the ladies of the Samurai class would compete with each other to embroider the most beautiful designs on the balls using silk threads. When the daughter of the Lord of the clan was married, the journey to her new home was often long and tedious. To while away the time she took her temari, known as *hime* (princess) *mari* or *goten* (castle) *mari*, with her on the journey. These amused her and gave her comfort as she moved away from her family.

At first, the making of temari was very much a hobby for the leisured classes, as they were the only ones who had access to the materials needed. By the nineteenth century, however, cotton became more easily available to the lower classes and the craft soon spread. Nineteenth century women utilised whatever materials were to hand, such as old clothes, weaving yarns and raw silk. Thrift has always featured in folk craft and temari is no exception.

The finished temari were popular as a girl's toy. They were used in mari games (*mari-tsuki*) and the children sang songs (*uta*) similar to our nursery rhymes, matching the movements of the balls to the music. Mothers made temari for their daughters and passed the craft on from one generation to another.

In the southern part of Japan, temari were used also as charms, and some of the designs were symbolic. Temari patterns were mainly geometric and the designs came from different parts of Japan. The way that the embroidery was worked varied also from place to place. Silk threads were not available to the lower classes, so they used short lengths of yarn tied together to make longer lengths. These could not be stitched, so the winding method was used to create the design, and this method is described later in the book, see pages 20, 43–50. Stitched designs are very popular now and any number of patterns can be developed.

With the introduction of the rubber ball, the craft of temari declined early in the twentieth century, but it made a comeback about twenty years ago. The Temari Association of Japan now has thousands of members including myself.

Temari is described as 'embroidering the surface of a ball'. *Te* means hand and *mari* means ball. The word for stitching is *kagari*. The basic ball is called a *dodai-mari*, or foundation mari, and this is formed in the way described later in the book, see pages 12–14.

It is some years now since I first saw the intriguing words 'embroidering the surface of a ball', and they set me off on a voyage of discovery that I still find quite fascinating. My tutor, Suzuko Anai, a Japanese lady married to an Englishman, had re-discovered this very ancient Japanese craft on a visit home to Fukuoka in South Japan. She was delighted to find her English friends so keen to learn, and was happy to share her knowledge with us.

Suzuko maintained that the surface of the round ball offers an almost infinite number of

A colourful selection of both simple and complex temari designs.

possibilities for the creation of beautiful patterns. In fact, the art of exploring colour and shape in relation to the divisions of the surface, with its large variety of combinations, has been well established already in patchwork. Just like patchwork, the craft of temari has much to offer us, especially in modern society where the importance of handicrafts is being revalued. This, I am sure, is how we manage to keep crafts alive, by sharing our knowledge and ideas with those who want to learn, and by encouraging people to experiment and try some of their own designs.

What can you do with temari? These days they are used mainly as decorations, for example, a few in a bowl or a group on a shelf. There are those who feel that there is no need to do anything else with them, but even the Japanese are finding new ways of using temari, such as in jewellery making. Like most embroidery techniques, temari can be developed in a tasteful way.

I am a great believer in crafts being enjoyable, even fun, and temari can certainly be that! You will agree, perhaps, when you find yourself on your hands and knees looking for a partially wound mari under a chair, or trying to get to it before the cat does. The smallest ones can seem to have a life of their own, but it all adds to the fun! Whatever your level of expertise, however, and your eventual intended purpose for the temari, I hope that you will enjoy exploring the delights of this ancient craft.

Equipment and materials

The equipment and materials needed to begin to explore the craft of temari are few and inexpensive. You will probably already have some of the following in your sewing kit.

Darning needles in various sizes

Tapestry needles, optional

Glass-headed pins

Mapping pins, useful where the basic mari is very firm and where longer pins cannot be used easily

Embroidery scissors and paper-cutting scissors

Tape measure

Narrow strips of paper long enough to measure the circumference of the mari, noting that newspaper is not suitable as it tears easily

Use any one of the following for the basic mari:

    Nylon tights or stockings

    Polystyrene beads, used for bean bags

    Soft polystyrene packaging

    Solid polystyrene balls

    Hollow polystyrene balls

    Cotton wool balls

    Toy stuffing inside polythene food bags

    Table tennis balls

    Wooden balls

Knitting wool, up to 4 ply

Reels of sewing thread in colours matching that of the knitting wool, noting that you do not need to use expensive thread

Embroidery threads, see pages 15–16

Beads and sequins, optional

Tinkle chimes and birdie chimes, optional

Bells or dried pulses, such as peas, can be used in hollow balls to make a noisy mari

Tassels, optional

Items used for making temari.

Colourful and exciting accessories can be produced by incorporating tiny temari with beads.

You can incorporate small temari into many different projects. Here, I have used three to decorate the lid of a box. This has been enhanced also by the use of gold embroidery and applique.

10

How to begin

How to begin

Before you can start creating a temari design you have to make a foundation mari on which to work. Then, you must select your embroidery threads, remembering that the colours and the type of thread that you choose will affect the finished design. Finally, you must prepare your basic mari by dividing and marking it into sections, the number of sections depending on the design that you plan to work.

Making the basic mari

You can use various types of material to make the basic foundation for a colourful mari. The choice of foundation will determine whether the mari is soft and light or firm and rigid.

If you find it difficult to start winding the wool because of the shiny surface of your base, such as plastic balls or table tennis balls, then use a small amount of double-sided sticky tape to anchor the end of your wool. Note also that if you use a base such as a wooden ball, plastic ball or table tennis ball, then pins will not go very far into your surface, and it is wise not to use this type of base for complex divisions. If you want to use tinkle chimes or birdie chimes inside a mari, then use the polystyrene beads method. These chimes are apt to move around, so care must be taken when wrapping.

You can experiment with fillings other than those described in this section, although I do not recommend dry oasis balls, such as those used for flower arranging, as they have a tendency to disintegrate.

Items used for temari bases.

Using tights or stockings

There are various ways of making a mari. The one that I was taught first, and which stays with the idea of thrift, was to utilise old (washed!) tights or stockings. The advantage of these is availability, as I am sure that I am not the only one to have a plentiful supply of tights full of ladders and holes. Also, they make a mari of good weight which is easy to handle. The main disadvantage, as many of my students have discovered, is getting a nice round ball. The tights may be cut into strips first, before winding into a ball. This takes a little longer but some of my students have found that they get a rounder ball this way. It takes a lot of practice, but here is the method:

1) Roll up one pair of tights from the foot end and tuck securely into the elasticated top to form a roundish shape, see Stage 1. You can use just one leg, or one stocking, for a smaller mari, or two or more pairs for a larger mari – the more that you use, the heavier the temari.

2) Cover this shape tightly with wool which must be wound 'every which way'. In other words, it must be wound in every direction, turning the ball all the time so that it covers evenly with no lumps. As you work, roll the mari regularly in your hands, or on a table, to get a really round shape, see Stage 2.

3) When covered satisfactorily, thread the end of the wool onto a darning needle, leaving a good length, and catch this down at intervals, before 'losing' the end of the wool inside the mari by pushing the darning needle inside and bringing it up as far as it will reach. Cut off the excess wool. You may prefer to use a large-eyed tapestry needle at this stage, as these can be easier to thread the wool through.

4) Repeat steps 2 and 3 with a matching shade

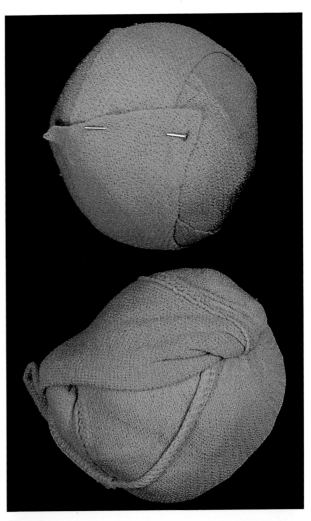

Stage 1

Stage 1 *Rolling the tights into a round shape. The smoother shape, above, has been formed using tights which have been cut into strips before rolling.*

Stage 2 *Wrapping the shape with wool.*

Stage 2

of sewing thread, see Stages 3 and 4. By using matching thread it does not matter if the mari is not covered too closely and some of the wool shows through.

Stage 3 *Covering the shape with thread. (A contrasting colour has been used solely for the purpose of easy viewing.)*

Stage 4 *The finished foundation mari.*

Using solid polystyrene balls

These are available in three sizes, 6.5 cm (2½ in), 4 cm (1½ in) and 2.5 cm (1 in). For the largest size, cover with wool and thread as given for the tights method. Smaller balls can be covered directly with thread. The main disadvantage with these is that you cannot push your needle through very far, so care must be taken when starting and finishing off the thread. Care must be taken also when wrapping with wool. Wool moulds itself round the softer bases, but air pockets are liable to form with all the harder bases and the base can become rather lumpy as a result.

Using hollow polystyrene balls

If you want to produce a noisy mari, then these can be filled with dried pulses, such as peas or lentils, or a bell can be placed inside, before covering as given for the tights method.

Using polystyrene beads

These are used for stuffing bean bags and are widely available. Cut off one foot from a pair of tights and stuff it with beads. This can be extended to whatever size you require and makes a very light temari with a good round shape. Cover as given for the tights method. Soft polystyrene packaging can be used in the same way.

Using cotton wool balls

These are widely available in various sizes. Cover as for solid polystyrene balls.

Using toy stuffing

Use any type of toy stuffing. Place the required amount in a polythene food bag and secure. Prick the bag to let out the air. Cover as given for the tights method.

Using table tennis balls

Cover as given for the tights method.

Using wooden balls

The large size makes a heavy temari. Cover as given for the tights method.

14

Colour

Colour is very important in the craft of temari, and the embroidery threads must be chosen with the background colour in mind. At this stage I would like to issue a *temari health warning*! Some background colours can 'kill' the colours of the embroidery threads. Some time ago, I spent hours perfecting a very complicated variation of the chrysanthemum design on a grey background, only to find that it was completely 'lost' when I had finished. Grey is a difficult colour on which to work, as are some dull pinks and greens. So be careful! The use of black, white or a shiny thread as an outline can often help to 'lift' a design. Choice of colours is very personal – I had one student who worked entirely in browns and yellows, whereas I have a personal preference for pinks, greens and mauves – but it is often a good idea to think where the temari might be placed and work in colours to blend with the decor.

For the purpose of making this book as bright and colourful as possible, I have managed to get away from personal preferences and use primary colours, and others, which I would not have used normally. I have been inspired especially by nature. On a recent holiday on the Isle of Anglesey I saw cliffs covered entirely with a vast carpet of mauve and purple heather, golden gorse and bright green ferns. I used these colours on my next temari and found my personal preferences widening all the time. I have been inspired also by colours used on fabrics. Just look around you – there is a vast sea of colour out there!

A selection of embroidery threads suitable for creating temari designs.

Embroidery threads

Once the basic mari has been made it must be divided and marked into sections before commencing the embroidery. The thread used will depend on the design chosen, and in some instances none of the marker threads will show once the design has been completed so there is no need to use an embroidery thread. A contrasting cotton thread which will show up on the surface of the temari can be used instead. On most temari the marker threads are incorporated as part of the design and you can use either one of the threads chosen for the main design, or a shiny metallic thread in gold or silver, or embroidery threads which incorporate a strand of glitter, depending on the effect that you require.

The most suitable embroidery threads are Perlé 8, Perlé 5 and Coton à Broder. These three have a good sheen, and Perlé 8 and Coton à Broder can be used together on the temari. Perlé 5 gives a slightly heavier look and is best used on its own. Perlé thread comes in a good range of random-dyed colours which are very attractive and give excellent results.

Threads comprising up to six individual strands may be used but a non-divisible thread is much better as it does not twist while working and gives a smoother look. You can use pure silk threads, but these are, of course, rather expensive, and some of the temari designs need a lot of thread. Shiny rayon threads are not very suitable as they have a tendency to 'slip'.

Beads and sequins

As far as I am aware, beads and sequins are not used on traditional Japanese temari but they can be useful for adding to blank spaces or covering a point which is not very neat! Sew them on with a thread to match the base. Bring the needle up at the required position and thread a sequin, and then a bead, onto the needle and down the thread. Take the thread down through the sequin so that the bead anchors the sequin in place. Lose the thread inside the mari by bringing the needle back up at any point away from the bead and cutting off the excess thread. If you are going to hang the temari up, then a tassel may be added.

Abbreviations

NP North Pole
SP South Pole
EQ Equator
PP Polar point, refers to the North and South Poles, or, as in the case of simple 4 division, to each point where the lines cross
FM Foundation mari
SD Simple division
CD Complex division

Dividing the basic mari

1) To divide the basic mari, you will need glass-headed pins so that they do not disappear into the base and a narrow strip of paper long enough to go round the mari.

2) Using one of the pins, secure the paper tape close to one end, at any point on the mari. This is called the North Pole, see Fig 1. Measure the circumference accurately by taking the tape right round the mari to meet back at the North Pole. Cut or tear off the excess.

3) Bend the tape back in half, leaving it anchored at the North Pole, and place another pin close to the fold of the tape at the opposite end of the mari. This is now the South Pole, see Fig 2.

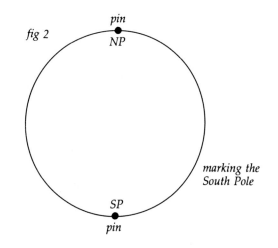

fig 2

marking the South Pole

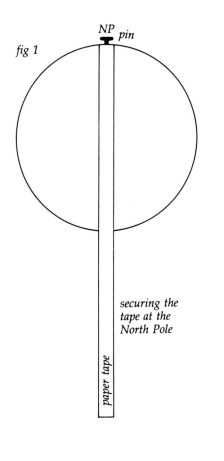

fig 1

securing the tape at the North Pole

paper tape

4) Bend the tape back again so that it is now in four quarters, and place four pins at regular intervals round the middle of the mari between the two poles, close to the folds of the tape. This is now the equator, see Fig 3.

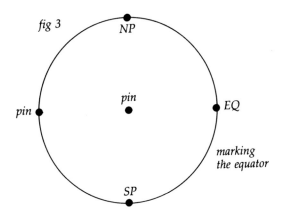

fig 3

marking the equator

5) Carefully pull the tape away from the mari and cut notches at each fold line, see Fig 4.

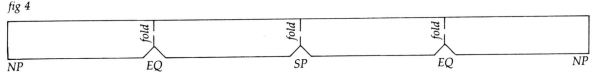

fig 4

cutting notches in the tape

17

6) Hold the tape round the equator and move the pins carefully to match each notch. They will now be equidistant.

7) You will need the paper tape again to produce some of the temari designs shown later in the book. Cut off one quarter of the tape and fold this in half. Cut a notch at the fold line. This will give you the point exactly halfway between a polar point and the equator. Keep this new paper tape pattern on one side.

Putting in the marker threads

1) Thread a darning needle with a good length of chosen thread. If using metallic thread, then make sure that the eye of the needle is large enough for it to go through easily or it may unravel. Insert the needle into the mari approximately 2.5 cm (1 in) or more away from the North Pole. Bring the needle up at the North Pole and pull the thread through until it just disappears into the base, see Fig 1.

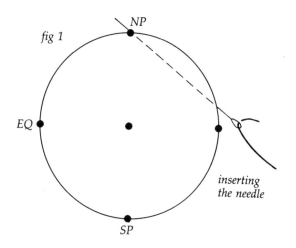

2) Being careful not to pull the thread, take it round to the South Pole via the equator, picking up a tiny amount of thread at the equator pins and the South Pole to anchor it. Do exactly the same round the other side, back to the North Pole. Push the needle through from the North Pole to any equator pin, and, if you find that you are unable to do this in one movement, then come up as far as you can and push the needle back in at the same point before continuing the journey to the equator, see Fig 2.

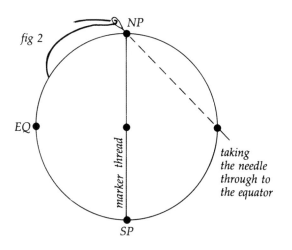

3) Take the thread round the equator in the same way. This is referred to as a simple 4 division.

4) To divide the mari into 8 or 16, fold the tape into the number of divisions required and follow the instructions given above. It is more difficult to fold the tape into 5, 6, and 10, and you may find it easier to measure accurately with a tape measure.

5) Marker threads may be removed on completion of the design if you are not happy with them, but traditionally they are left in place.

Simple temari designs

Simple temari designs

Designs for the mari can be achieved by one of two methods. You may create a solid pattern either by wrapping or with herringbone stitch. The spaces between the solid patterns can be linked with a series of straight stitches.

Wrapping

Simply wind the thread round the mari to produce a wrapped design (*maki kagari*). The only stitching used is to hold the threads in place when necessary.

Stitching

The only stitch used for solid patterns is herringbone stitch (*chidori kagari*), see Figs 1 and 2.

For filling in spaces, pineneedle stitch (*matsuba kagari*) is often used. This is a series of straight stitches and can be used in various ways, see Figs 3, 4 and 5.

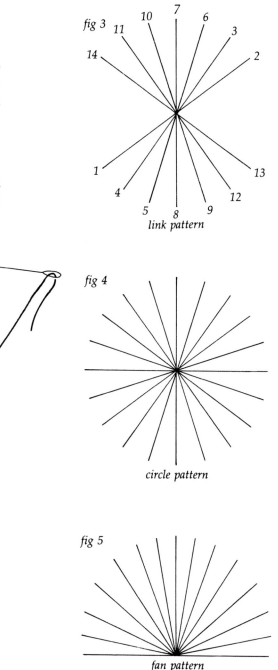

fig 3

link pattern

fig 1

working herringbone stitch

fig 2

herringbone stitch as a solid pattern

fig 4

circle pattern

fig 5

fan pattern

Simple division

A wide range of colourful patterns can be created using simple division. The designs described on the following pages use 4 SD, 6 SD, 8 SD and 10 SD.

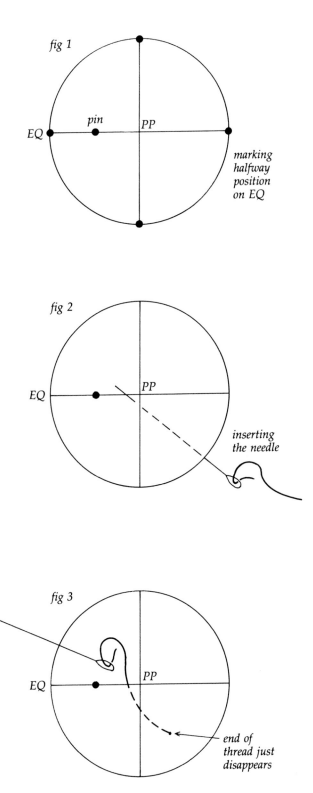

fig 1

marking halfway position on EQ

A close-up showing details of a square design.

Squares

1) Divide the FM into 4 SD, using a contrasting cotton thread. The marker threads will be covered completely in this design.

2) Using the paper tape pattern, place a pin at the point halfway between the PP and the EQ, on any one marker thread, see Fig 1. Push it right in unless you are using a hard base, such as a wooden ball or a solid polystyrene ball. In this case just push it in as far as you are able, or try using a mapping pin.

3) Thread a darning needle with the chosen thread and push it into the mari 2.5 cm (1 in) or more away from the PP, see Fig 2. Bring the needle through at the PP to the left of the marker thread, losing the end of the thread inside the mari. Be careful not to pull the thread hard, see Fig 3.

fig 2

inserting the needle

fig 3

end of thread just disappears

4) Working clockwise, and using herringbone stitches, complete a square until it reaches the marker pin, changing your colours as required. Pick up only a tiny amount of the base thread when working the stitch, see Figs 4 and 5. If you put a pin at the EQ on the marker thread on which you commence working the design, then you will know each time that you have completed the four sides of the square, see Fig 6.

5) Work squares at each PP. They will automatically reach the point of the adjacent square and no marker pin is required after the first square.

6) Fill in with a 'Y' pattern of straight stitches (*Y kagari*). Take a thread across from the centre of one triangle to the centre of another, crossing the point where two corners of a square meet, see Fig 7.

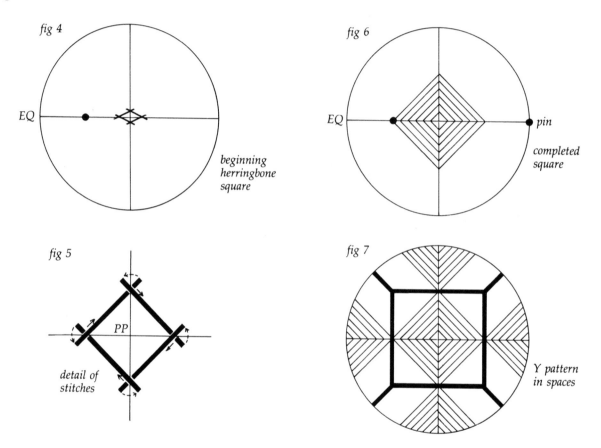

fig 4

EQ

beginning herringbone square

fig 6

EQ

pin

completed square

fig 5

PP

detail of stitches

fig 7

Y pattern in spaces

Opposite: *a colourful selection of square designs.*

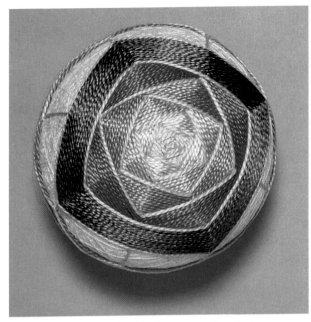

A close-up showing details of a rose garden design.

Rose garden

1) This is a very attractive variation of the squares design and is worked at the NP and the SP only. Divide the FM into 8 SD.

2) Using four alternate marker threads, work a small square, see Fig 1. This design looks best when worked in shades of one colour with a contrast in the centre.

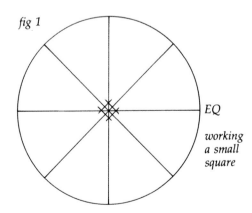

fig 1

EQ

working a small square

3) Using the other alternating marker threads, work another square, crossing and covering the corners of the previous one.

4) Continue in this way until approximately 1 cm (½ in) from the EQ, see Fig 2.

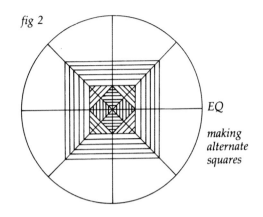

fig 2

EQ

making alternate squares

5) Bring a threaded needle up anywhere to one side of the EQ marker thread. Wind the thread round the mari, parallel to the EQ, as many times as required. Do the same on the other side of the marker thread. Hold down the threads with herringbone stitches, see Fig 3.

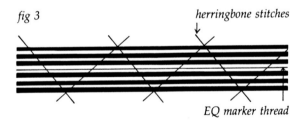

fig 3

herringbone stitches

EQ marker thread

Opposite: *a colourful selection of rose garden designs.*

Spindles

1) Divide the FM into 8 SD.

2) You do not need to put a marker thread round the EQ, but leave the EQ pins in place when you have divided the temari.

3) Place a marker pin at the point halfway between the PP and the EQ at both ends of one of the marker threads, see Fig 1. Place a pin at the PP at which you commence working. You will know then each time that you have worked both sides of the spindle.

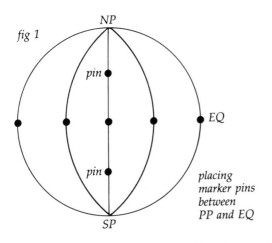

fig 1

placing marker pins between PP and EQ

4) Bring the thread up to the left of a marker pin, see Fig 2. Take it across to the right of the EQ pin, and, turning the mari, push the needle in from right to left at the opposite marker pin, see Fig 3. Take the thread back to the beginning in the same way, see Fig 4.

5) Picking up only a small amount of the base thread, work towards the PP. Use your thumb to smooth the threads as the spindles grow

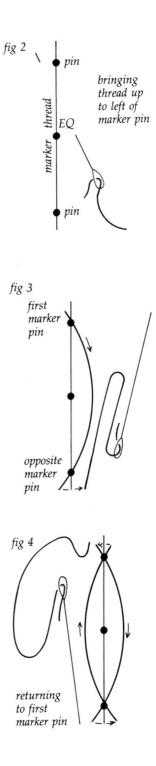

fig 2

bringing thread up to left of marker pin

marker thread

EQ

pin

pin

fig 3

first marker pin

opposite marker pin

fig 4

returning to first marker pin

Opposite: *a colourful selection of spindle designs.*

27

A close-up showing details of a spindle design.

A close-up showing details of an interlocking spindle design.

A close-up showing details of a crossed spindle design.

28

wider. Change colour as required. You can remove the marker pins when you have the first complete spindle in place. Leave the EQ pins in place until you have worked a few rows.

6) Work spindles on each marker thread.

7) Work straight stitches across the PPs.

Crossed spindles

1) This is a variation of the spindles design. Divide the FM into 4 SD.

2) You will need to work with two needles for this design, threaded with different colours. If you divide the FM into 8 SD, then you can work four crossed spindles across the PP, using four needles and four colours.

3) Place a marker pin at the point halfway between the PP and the EQ on all four marker threads. You will work across the PPs only at each end.

4) Work spindles, as described on page 27, steps 4 and 5, but using the different coloured threads alternately. Firstly, work a spindle from A to B, and then cross over this by working a spindle from C to D, see Fig 1. Continue in this way until approximately 1 cm (½ in) from the EQ, see Fig 2.

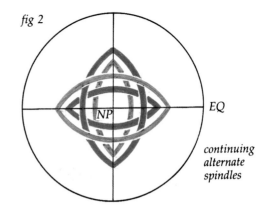

fig 2

continuing
alternate
spindles

5) Work straight stitches in the spaces and wrap the EQ, as given for rose garden step 5.

Interlocking spindles

1) Divide the FM into 6 SD.

2) You will need three colours for this design. Random-dyed threads work very well.

3) Working at the PP, place a pin at the point halfway between the PP and the EQ on all the marker threads, see Fig 1.

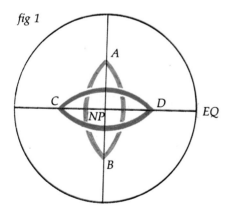

fig 1

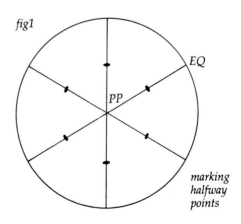

fig1

marking
halfway
points

29

4) Work a full spindle from A to B, see Fig 2.

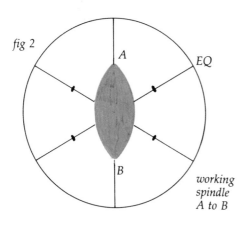

fig 2

working spindle A to B

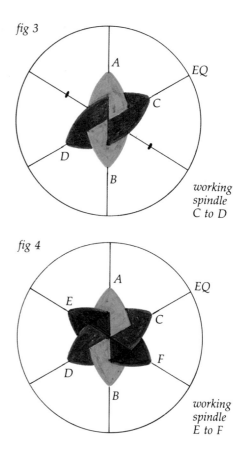

fig 3

working spindle C to D

fig 4

working spindle E to F

5) Work another spindle from C to D. Starting at C, take the thread over the first half of spindle AB and under the other half, to reach D. Return from D to C in a similar manner, taking the thread over the first half of spindle AB and under the other. Use the eye end of the needle to take the thread underneath the threads of spindle AB, see Fig 3. Continue working in this way until spindle CD is complete.

6) Work a third spindle from E to F. Starting at E, take the thread over the first halves of spindles AB and CD and under the other halves, to reach F. Return from F to E in a similar manner, see Fig 4. Continue working in this way until spindle EF is complete and all three spindles interlock.

7) Work in the same way at the opposite PP.

8) Work straight stitches in the spaces and wrap the EQ, as given for rose garden step 5.

Opposite: *a colourful selection of crossed and interlocking spindle designs.*

A close-up showing details of a three wing and hexagon design.

Three wing and hexagon

1) Divide the FM into 6 SD.
2) Work a small hexagon of about five or six rows at one PP, see Fig 1.
3) Put a marker pin at the point halfway between the PP and the EQ on three alternate marker threads only.
4) Bring the thread up at A. Take it across to B, then from B to C, from C to D, from D to E, from E to F, and from F back to A, see Fig 2. Continue in this way until the EQ is reached, changing colours as required. Put a pin at the EQ below point A so that you will know when each journey has been completed.
5) Work in the same way at the opposite PP, using the other alternating marker threads if you wish.
6) Work herringbone stitches across the EQ so that the threads cross. Work straight stitches over these points, see Fig 3.

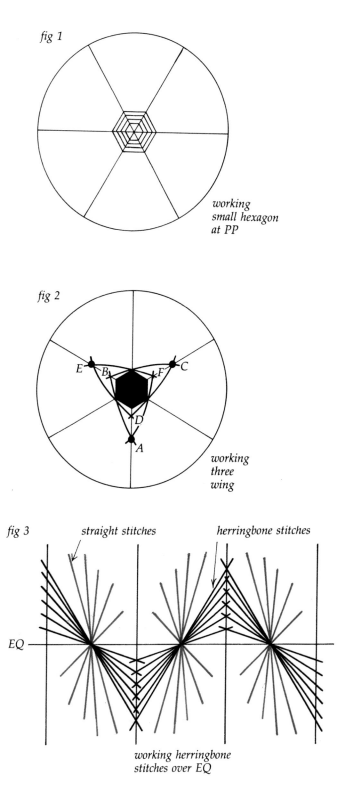

fig 1

working small hexagon at PP

fig 2

working three wing

fig 3   straight stitches   herringbone stitches

EQ

working herringbone stitches over EQ

Opposite: *a colourful selection of three wing and hexagon designs.*

33

A close-up showing details of a three wing design.

Three wing (minus the hexagon)

1) Divide the FM into 6 SD.

2) Random-dyed threads work well on this design, or you can use two or three colours, changing as required.

3) Put a marker pin at the point halfway between the PP and the EQ on three alternate marker threads.

4) Bring the thread up at point A and take it across to the PP on marker thread B. Then, take it down to point C, up to the PP on marker thread A, down to point B, up to the PP on marker thread C, and finally back to point A, see Fig 1.

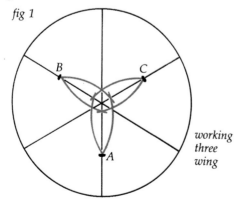

fig 1

working three wing

5) On the second and subsequent rows, take the needle under and over each wing to achieve the interlocking effect, see Fig 2. Remember to push the eye end of the needle under the threads.

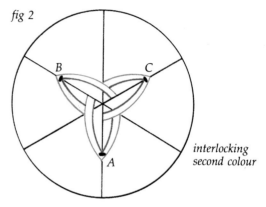

fig 2

interlocking second colour

6) Outline with a contrasting thread.

7) Work another three wing at the opposite end of the temari.

8) Work crossed spindles, squares, or any of the other 4 SD designs shown in the book, at the three cross sections on the EQ. Use a contrasting or matching thread.

Opposite: *a colourful selection of three wing designs.*

34

Pentagon

1) Divide the FM into 10 SD.

2) Put a marker pin at the point halfway between the PP and the EQ on five alternate marker threads.

3) Bring the thread up at A. Take it across to B, then from B to C, from C to D, from D to E, and from E back to A, see Fig 1. Make sure that you know at which point you started by placing a marker pin at the EQ on that thread.

4) Continue in the same way, changing the thread as you wish.

5) Work a pentagon at the opposite end of the temari.

6) You can either wrap the EQ, as given for rose garden step 5, or work herringbone stitches, see Fig 2. Work straight stitches across the PPs.

7) You can vary this design by working the pentagons on opposite alternating threads. A different pattern can be made by working a close pentagon at the PP, as given for three wing and hexagon step 2, and then continuing as from step 3 of this section.

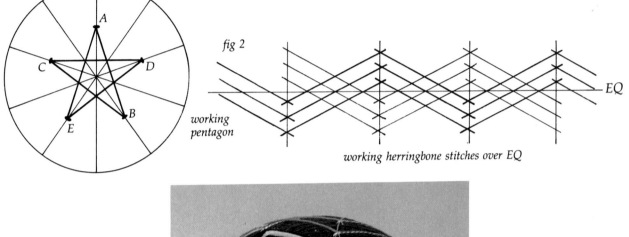

fig 1

fig 2

working pentagon

working herringbone stitches over EQ

EQ

Above: *a close-up showing details of a pentagon design.*

Opposite: *a colourful selection of pentagon designs.*

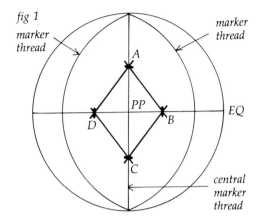

A close-up showing details of an interlocking diamond design.

Interlocking diamonds

1) Divide the FM into 8 SD.

2) Place a marker pin at the point halfway between the PP and the EQ at both ends of each marker thread.

3) Bring the thread up at A and take it across to B, which is the point on the EQ halfway between the central marker thread and the marker thread to the right. From B take the thread across to C and then to D, which is the point on the EQ halfway between the central marker thread and the marker thread to the left, see Fig 1.

4) Continue in this way until the diamond reaches the outer marker threads. Change colour as required.

5) Do exactly the same on each marker thread but work over and then under the previous diamond. Remember to push the eye end of the needle under the threads, see Fig 2.

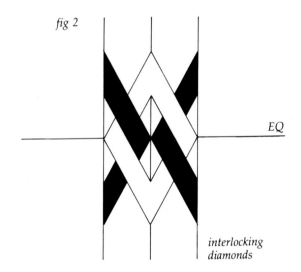

6) Work straight stitches across the PPs.

7) A variation of this design is woven diamonds. Thread two needles with different coloured threads. Work the diamonds one row at a time, first one colour and then the next. Continue in this way round the temari until the outer marker threads for each diamond have been reached.

Opposite: *a colourful selection of interlocking diamond designs.*

Chrysanthemum

1) Divide the FM into 8 SD.

2) Place a marker pin at the point halfway between the PP and the EQ on each marker thread.

3) Bring the thread up near the PP on marker thread A. Then, take it down to point B, up to the PP on marker thread C, down to point D, up to the PP on marker thread E, down to point F, up to the PP on marker thread G, down to point H, and finally back to the PP on marker thread A, see Fig 1.

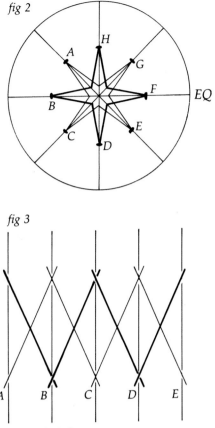

fig 2

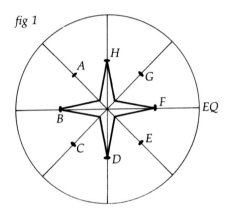

fig 1

fig 3

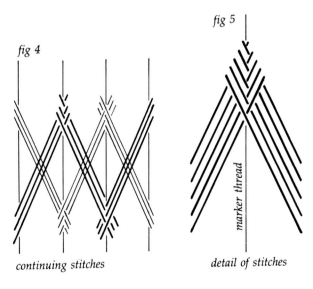

detail of stitches

4) Slip the needle through to the PP on marker thread B. Then, take it down to point C, up to the PP on marker thread D, down to point E, up to the PP on marker thread F, down to point G, up to the PP on marker thread H, down to point A, and finally back to the PP on marker thread B, see Figs 2 and 3.

5) Continue in this way, alternating steps 3 and 4 and making each stitch slightly wider as you work. Change colour as required, see Figs 4 and 5.

fig 4

fig 5

continuing stitches

detail of stitches

marker thread

Opposite: *a colourful selection of chrysanthemum designs.*

41

6) Work another chrysanthemum at the opposite end of the temari.

7) Wrap the EQ, as given for rose garden step 5.

8) This is probably one of the most popular temari designs and is one of my own personal favourites. The variations are numerous and here are just a few ideas. I am sure that you will be able to think of others.

• Try varying the length of each petal.

• Make a large temari and divide it into 16 or even 32. This gives more scope for varying petal lengths.

• Make the petals dovetail into those of the opposite chrysanthemum.

• Use two colours and work steps 3 and 4 separately. Weave over and under.

• Work the chrysanthemum from top to bottom. Take care with this as the lines cross each other at the EQ, see Fig 6.

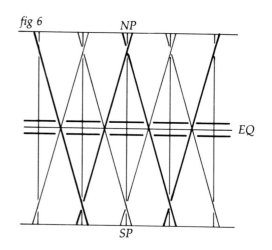

A close-up showing details of a chrysanthemum design.

Wrapped designs

Some very attractive patterns can be achieved by wrapping, and instructions are given here for just a few of them. When you have tried these designs, you can experiment with some variations of your own.

Design 1

1) Divide the FM into 4 SD.
2) You will need three colours for this temari. Using the first colour, bring the thread up near any PP and wind it round one side of the marker thread three times. Slip the needle under the marker thread and wrap the thread three times round the other side.
3) Repeat step 2 on the other two marker threads, crossing over at the PPs.
4) Using the second colour, return to the first marker thread and wrap three more rows on each side of the first colour. Repeat this on the other two marker threads, as given in step 3.
5) Using the third colour, repeat as given for the second colour in step 4.
6) Using either the second colour or a contrasting thread, outline each line with one or two rows, working as before.
7) Fill in the spaces with straight stitches.

A close-up showing details of a wrapped design, method 1.

43

A colourful selection of wrapped designs, method 1.

A colourful selection of wrapped designs, method 2.

Design 2

1) Divide the FM into 8 SD.

2) You will need two colours for this design. Bring the thread up at the NP and wrap four rows round one side of a marker thread. Repeat on the other side of the marker thread.

3) Repeat step 2 on each marker thread, crossing over at the PPs.

4) Return to the first marker thread, and, using a contrasting thread, wrap three more rows round each side of the first colour.

5) Repeat step 4 on each marker thread.

6) Wrap the EQ, as given for rose garden step 5. If you prefer, then work straight stitches across each PP.

A close-up showing details of a wrapped design, method 2.

Design 3

1) Divide the FM into 4 SD.

2) You will need at least two colours for this temari. Bring the thread up at any PP on the EQ. Wrap the thread round each side of the marker thread but crossing over at the PP each time, so that the wrapped threads form a bump, see Fig 1. It is best to leave a pin in at the PPs to prevent the threads from slipping, see Fig 2.

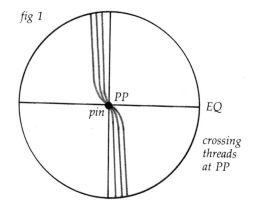

fig 1

PP

pin

EQ

crossing
threads
at PP

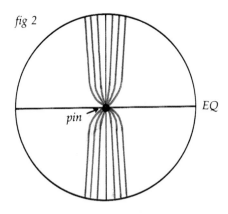

fig 2

pin

EQ

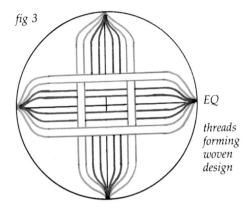

5) Using an outline thread, repeat steps 2 and 3 again, see Fig 3.

fig 3

EQ

threads forming woven design

3) Bring the thread up at one of the other PPs on the EQ and repeat step 2. The threads will cross each other at the NP and the SP, forming a woven design.

4) Repeat steps 2 and 3 using a contrasting thread.

6) Wrap the EQ, as given for rose garden step 5, working over and under the bumps to hold them in place. Work herringbone stitches over the EQ threads.

A close-up showing details of a wrapped design, method 3.

*A colourful selection
of wrapped designs,
method 3.*

A colourful selection of wrapped designs, method 4.

Design 4

1) Divide the FM into 4 SD.

2) Put a marker pin at the point halfway between the NP and the EQ, and the SP and the EQ, on all the marker threads.

3) For this design, a random-dyed thread is very attractive. Make sure that you have plenty of thread before you start as it uses a large amount.

4) Bring the thread up at any PP on the EQ. Take the thread round the FM, starting just inside the marker pins and working inwards towards the NP and the SP. Cross the threads over at the EQ to form a bump, as given for design 3 step 2. Work four rows, see Fig 1.

5) Repeat step 4 using your second colour and the other two PPs on the EQ.

6) Working four rows of each colour at a time, alternate steps 4 and 5 until the design is filled in and covers both the NP and the SP, see Fig 2.

7) Wrap the EQ, as given for rose garden step 5.

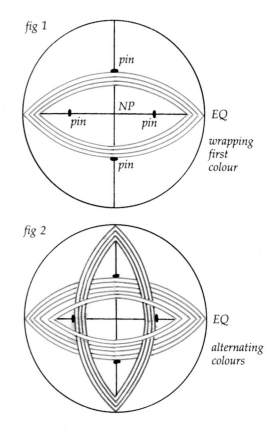

A close-up showing details of a wrapped design, method 4.

Complex
temari designs

Complex temari designs

Now that you have mastered simple division, I hope that you will feel competent enough to try your hand at complex division. Many of the designs that you have learnt already can be used on complex temari as you will see from the following pages. For basic details on stitching and wrapping techniques, see page 20.

Eight complex division

By dividing the basic mari into more sections you can achieve more complicated designs. The first of these complex divisions is based on a mari divided into 8 SD, referred to as 8 CD.

Dividing into eight sections

1) Divide the FM into 8 SD.
2) Place pins at alternate points on the EQ, see Fig 1.

3) Bring the marker thread up at A and take it round the FM to B, then back to A. Repeat in the opposite direction so that now you have two more opposite points where eight threads cross, see Fig 2.

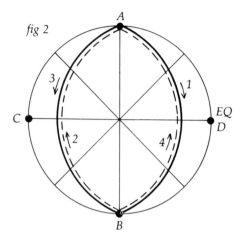

fig 2

4) Repeat the same process from C to D. Now you should have a FM with six points where eight threads cross. You will notice also that other shapes have appeared, giving you places where four and six threads cross, see Fig 3.

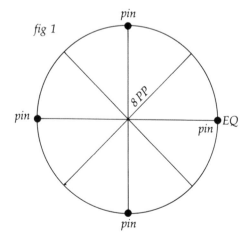

fig 1

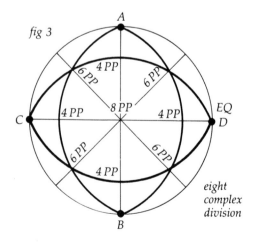

fig 3

eight complex division

52

A colourful selection of 8CD rose garden and chrysanthemum designs.

Rose garden

1) Divide the FM into 8 CD.
2) Work rose garden design at each 8 PP, see pages 24–25.
3) You may either fill in the triangles using herringbone stitches, or work three wing and hexagon or any other design of your choice.

Chrysanthemum

1) Divide the FM into 8 CD.
2) Work chrysanthemum design at each 8 PP, see pages 40–42.
3) Stitch both sides of the surrounding marker threads.

Three wing and hexagon

1) Divide the FM into 8 CD.
2) Work three wing and hexagon design at each 6 PP, see pages 32–33.
3) Work any design of your choice across each 8 PP or wrap threads across the 8 PPs in two directions.

Wrapped designs

1) Attractive temari can be made simply by wrapping threads on each side of the complex marker threads.
2) This design works well also on 10 complex division.

A close-up showing details of an 8CD interlocking triangle design.

Interlocking triangles

1) Divide the FM into 8 CD.

2) Wrap both sides of the three marker threads which outline the eight triangular shapes on the FM. Each triangular shape has an 8 PP at each of its three corners and a 6 PP in its centre, see Fig 1. Two of the three wrapped threads will cross at each 8 PP.

3) Using a contrasting thread, bring the thread up at A, take it across to B, then to C, and return to A. Work a triangle of the desired width, changing colour where necessary, see Fig 2.

4) Do exactly the same across each of the eight triangular shapes outlined by the wrapped marker threads. Interlock the triangles by working the threads over and under each other, see Fig 3. Do not forget to use the eye end of the needle to pass under the threads.

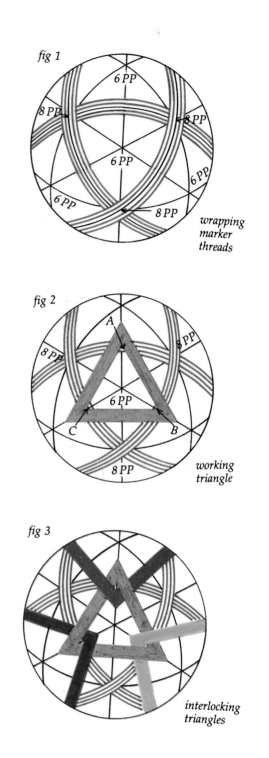

fig 1

wrapping marker threads

fig 2

working triangle

fig 3

interlocking triangles

Opposite: *a colourful selection of 8CD interlocking triangle designs.*

A close-up showing details of an 8CD woven square design.

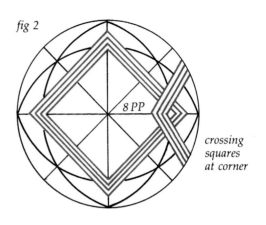

fig 2

8 PP

crossing squares at corner

4) Do the same at each 8 PP.

5) Return to the first square and repeat steps 2, 3 and 4 using the second colour. If you wish, then you may outline each colour with black, white, gold or silver.

6) Repeat steps 2, 3 and 4 again using the third colour.

7) Either work straight stitches across each 8 PP or use any other design of your choice, such as chrysanthemum or crossed spindles.

Woven squares

1) Divide the FM into 8 CD. Place a different coloured pin at each 8 PP and make a note of the one with which you start. Use at least three colours for this design.

2) Work a square from A to B to C to D using one of the colours. Four rows should be sufficient, see Fig 1.

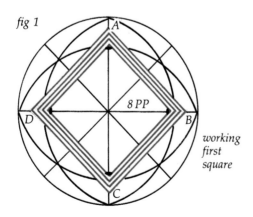

fig 1

A

D   8 PP   B

C

working first square

3) Using the same colour, work another square in the same way, crossing the first square at one corner, see Fig 2.

Opposite: *a colourful selection of 8CD woven square designs.*

56

Ten complex division

This is a very complicated division based on a mari divided into 10 SD and is referred to as 10 CD. In order to achieve this division it is imperative that the FM is *very* round.

Dividing into ten sections

1) Divide the FM into 10 SD *without* an EQ. Take five pins of five different colours, for example, black, red, blue, white and yellow, and place each one on a marker thread at the EQ line. Take another five pins, of the same five colours, and place these on the remaining marker threads, in the same colour sequence as before, see Stage 1.

2) Cut a paper tape exactly half the measurement of the circumference of the FM. Fold the tape into three and cut notches at each fold.

3) Place the top of the tape at the PP and, using the pins on the EQ, move them up to match the notch on the tape on alternate marker threads. Repeat at the opposite end of the mari on the other alternating threads. You will see now that each coloured pin is exactly opposite the one of the same colour. Each pin should be a third of the way down from the PP, and the measurement between each pin should also be one third of the measurement of the paper tape, see Stage 2.

4) To make ten divisions at each pin, choose any pin, for example, yellow, to start with. Bring the thread up at a yellow pin and take it round to the opposite yellow pin via a pin of any other colour, for example, blue, picking up a tiny amount of thread at each pin. Return, via the other blue pin, to the yellow pin at which you started, see Stage 3. Do the same using each coloured pin until ten divisions have been created at the new yellow PP. Remove the yellow pins. You will have put some marker threads at the other new PPs already as you went round this first time.

5) Choose another coloured pin and repeat step 4. Remove the pins each time that you finish a new PP. Continue in this way until all the pins have been removed and you have a FM with twelve divisions of ten and divisions of six and four, as in 8 CD, see Stage 4.

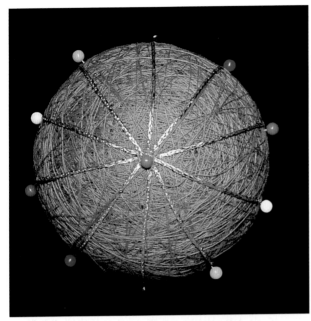

Stage 1 *Placing coloured pins at the EQ line.*

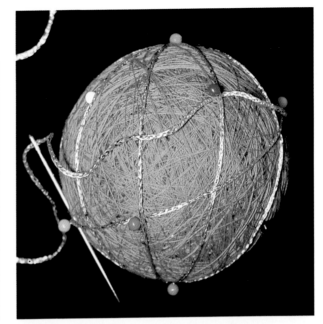

Stage 3 *Creating ten divisions at the yellow pin.*

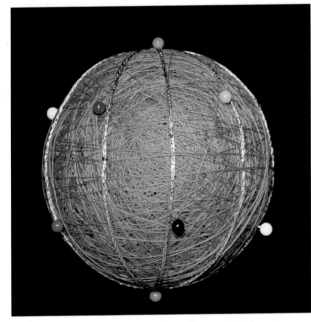

Stage 2 *Moving the pins along the marker threads.*

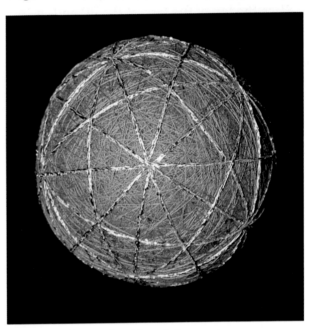

Stage 4 *The completed foundation mari, divided into 10CD.*

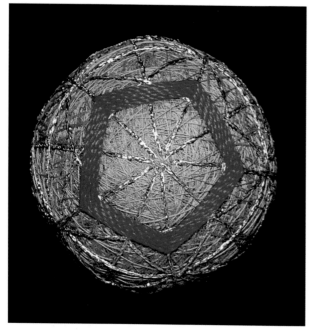

Interlocking pentagons

1) Divide the FM into 10 CD.

2) Work a pentagon at a 10 PP, using the marker threads where only two threads cross and working outside the pentagon shape outlined by these threads, see Stage 1. Six rows should be sufficient but more may be added later if you wish. Change colour as required.

3) Do the same at each 10 PP, working inside the adjacent pentagon and working over and under where each one meets, see Stage 2.

4) Work straight stitches across each 10 PP.

Stage 1 *Working the first pentagon.*

A close-up showing details of a 10CD interlocking pentagon design.

Stage 2 *Interlocking the second pentagon.*

Opposite: *a colourful selection of 10CD interlocking pentagon designs.*

A colourful selection of 10CD chrysanthemum and rose garden designs.

Chrysanthemum

1) Divide the FM into 10 CD.
2) Work chrysanthemum design at each 10 PP, see pages 40–42.
3) Either stitch both sides of the surrounding marker threads or work three wing and hexagon at each 6 PP.

Rose garden

1) Divide the FM into 10 CD.
2) Work rose garden design at each 10 PP, see pages 24–25, and finish with outer rows of a darker colour.

Complex variations based on a foundation mari divided into 10CD.

I hope that you have enjoyed making the designs
shown in this book and that now you will feel able
to try creating some of your own,
either by experimenting with the techniques described
or simply by varying the designs that
you have learnt already.

Index

Abbreviations 16

Balls
    cotton wool 9, 14
    plastic 12
    polystyrene 9, 14
    table tennis 9, 12, 14
    wooden 9, 12, 14
Basic mari 12–18
Beads 9, 14, 16

Chimes 9, 12
Chrysanthemum 40–42, 53, 62
Colour 15
Complex temari designs 52–63
Crossed spindles 28–29, 31

Darning needles 9, 13, 18
Designs
    complex 52–63
    simple 20–42
    wrapped 43–50, 53
Diamonds, interlocking 38–39
Dividing the basic mari 17–18
Divisions
    eight complex 52–57
    simple 17–18, 21–42
    ten complex 58–63

Eight complex division 52–57
Embroidery threads 9, 15–16
Equator 17
Equipment and materials 9

Foundation mari 12

Glass-headed pins 9

Herringbone stitch 20
How to begin 12–18

Interlocking diamonds 38–39
Interlocking pentagons 60–61
Interlocking spindles 28–31
Interlocking triangles 54–55

Kagari 6
Kemari 6
Knitting wool 9, 12–13

Mapping pins 9
Mari 6
Mari, basic 12–18
Marker threads 18

Needles
    darning 9, 13, 18
    tapestry 9
North Pole 17

Paper tape 9, 17–18
Pentagon 36–37, 60–61
Pins 9, 12
    glass-headed 9
    mapping 9
Polar point 16
Pulses 9

Rose garden 24–25, 53, 62

Scissors 9
Sequins 9, 16
Simple division 17–18, 21–42
Simple temari designs 20–42
South Pole 17
Spindles 26–31
    crossed 28–29, 31
    interlocking 29–31
Squares 21–23, 56–57
Stitches
    herringbone 20
    straight 20
Stockings 9, 13
Stuffing, toy 9, 14

Tape
    measure 9, 18
    paper 9, 17–18
Tapestry needles 9
Tassels 9
Ten complex division 58–63
Thread 9
Three wing and hexagon 32–33, 53
Three wing (minus hexagon) 34–35
Tights 9, 13
Toy stuffing 9, 14
Triangles, interlocking 54–55

Wool, knitting 9, 12–13
Woven squares 56–57
Wrapped designs 43–50, 53
Wrapping 20
Wrapping the equator 25

If readers have difficulty in obtaining any of the materials
or equipment mentioned in this book,
please write for further information to the publishers,
Search Press Ltd., Wellwood, North Farm Road,
Tunbridge Wells, Kent, TN2 3DR